DEDICATION

To the next generation of technologists who blend creativity and technical rigor to build an inclusive, innovative digital future.

FOREWORD

In a world where technology evolves daily, mastering computer applications requires both a strong foundation and a forward-looking perspective. This book, born from my experience and building software, offers a unique, hands-on guide to software development, AI, and emerging fields like agentic AI, post-quantum cryptography, spatial computing, quantum computing, and sustainable IT. Designed for students, self-learners, and professionals, it blends core concepts with practical projects, ethical considerations, and 2025 trends—such as AI governance platforms, 6G networks, and biotechnology integration—to prepare you for roles like software developer, AI engineer, or cloud architect. With accessible tools and inclusive practices, this guide is your partner in shaping the digital future.

FOUNDATIONS AND FRONTIERS OF COMPUTING

A Comprehensive Guide to Software Development, AI, and Emerging Technologies

BY ATUL SINGH
(PEN NAME: SHYAMANKAR SINGHARI)

First Edition — 2025
For permissions, inquiries, or educational use requests, contact: contact@wkrishind.in

TABLE OF CONTENTS

INTRODUCTION

Foundations and Frontiers of Computing is a transformative guide to mastering computer applications, crafted from my decade-long experience teaching at technical institutes and contributing to industry projects. Unlike generic textbooks, this book synthesizes a unique curriculum that balances foundational skills (e.g., programming in C and Python) with cutting-edge topics (e.g., agentic AI, post-quantum cryptography, quantum basics) tailored for 2025's tech landscape.

No external courses are needed—just a computer (Windows, Mac, or Linux) with internet access for setup. Key features include:

- **Practical Focus**: Original code in C, Python, Java, with projects like a custom Library Management System.

- **Inclusivity**: Accessibility tools (e.g., screen reader support in VS Code) and ethical AI discussions.
- **2025 Alignment**: Covers AI automation, quantum computing, blockchain, green computing, spatial computing, and 6G integration.
- **Portfolio Building**: Exercises and projects to create a professional portfolio.

Start coding, practice daily, and build your future in tech with this all-in-one resource.

Part 1:

FOUNDATIONS IN COMPUTING

PREFACE TO PART 1

Part 1 lays the groundwork for your tech journey, introducing programming (C and Python), data structures, discrete mathematics, computer architecture, and databases, with an elective in web technologies. Designed for beginners, it emphasizes hands-on learning with projects inspired by real classroom experiences, ensuring accessibility for all learners.

Chapter 0

SETTING UP YOUR PROGRAMMING ENVIRONMENT

Set up a robust environment for coding and learning, updated for 2025 tools.

Step 1: Install a Code Editor

Tool: Visual Studio Code (VS Code) – Free, cross-platform.

Download: https://code.visualstudio.com/.

Extensions: C/C++, Python (with Pylance for enhanced intelligence), SQLTools, Live Server (for Web Tech elective), autoDocstring for Python docstrings.

Step 2: Install Compilers/Interpreters

C: Install GCC.

Windows: MinGW (https://www.mingw-w64.org/).

Mac: Homebrew (brew install gcc after installing https://brew.sh/).
Linux: sudo apt install gcc (Ubuntu).
Python: Python 3.13.7 (latest as of September 2025, https://www.python.org/).
Libraries: pip install numpy pandas.
DBMS: SQLite (built-in with Python) or MySQL 8.0.44 (https://dev.mysql.com/downloads/).
Web Tech: Chrome/Firefox for HTML/CSS/JS testing.

Step 3: Version Control

Install Git: https://git-scm.com/.
Create a GitHub account for project storage.

Step 4: Test Setup

C Test:

```
#include <stdio.h>

int main() {
```

```
    printf("Hello, C! Ready for 2025 computing.\n");

    return 0;

}
```

Save as hello.c, compile: gcc hello.c -o hello, run: ./hello (Linux/Mac) or hello.exe (Windows).
Output: Hello, C! Ready for 2025 computing.

Python Test:

```
print("Hello, Python! Exploring 2025 trends.")
```

Save as hello.py, run: python hello.py.
Output: Hello, Python! Exploring 2025 trends.

SQL Test (SQLite):

```
import sqlite3
```

```
conn = sqlite3.connect(':memory:')

cursor = conn.cursor()

cursor.execute("CREATE TABLE test (id
INTEGER, name TEXT)")

cursor.execute("INSERT INTO test
VALUES (1, 'Test')")

cursor.execute("SELECT * FROM test")

print(cursor.fetchall())  # [(1, 'Test')]
```

Tips: Use terminals like iTerm2 (Mac) or PowerShell (Windows). Enable VS Code’s accessibility mode (e.g., screen reader support) for inclusivity.

Chapter 1

PROGRAMMING FUNDAMENTALS (C AND PYTHON)

This chapter introduces programming through C (for low-level control) and Python (for versatility), with examples drawn from my teaching to make complex concepts approachable.

1.1 Introduction to C

C is the backbone of system programming, offering insights into memory and performance. Let's start with a program inspired by a student project I mentored—a simple grade calculator for a classroom.

1.1.1 Basics and Data Types

C uses fixed data types: `int` (4 bytes), `float` (4 bytes), `char` (1 byte), `double`

(8 bytes). Variables must be declared before use.

Example: Classroom Grade Calculator

```
#include <stdio.h>

int main() {

   int marks = 85;

   float percentage = (marks / 100.0) * 100;

      printf("Student Marks: %d, Percentage: %.2f%%\n", marks, percentage);

   return 0;

}
```

Output: Student Marks: 85, Percentage: 85.00%

This program, inspired by a student's need to automate grade reports, calculates a percentage from raw marks.

1.1.2 Control Structures

Control structures guide program flow. For example, a grading system:

```
#include <stdio.h>

int main() {

    int marks = 85;

    if (marks >= 90) {

        printf("Grade: A+\n");

    } else if (marks >= 80) {

        printf("Grade: A\n");

    } else {

        printf("Grade: B or below\n");

    }

    return 0;

}
```

Output: Grade: A

This reflects a real-world grading logic I used in classroom exercises.

1.1.3 Functions

Functions modularize code. Here's a function to compute a student's total marks:

```
#include <stdio.h>

int total_marks(int subject1, int subject2) {

    return subject1 + subject2;

}

int main() {

    int math = 45, science = 50;

                printf("Total Marks: %d\n",
total_marks(math, science));

    return 0;

}
```

Output: Total Marks: 95

This function mirrors a utility I created for quick grading during exams.

1.1.4 Arrays and Strings

Arrays store multiple values, like a list of student IDs:

```
#include <stdio.h>

int main() {

   int student_ids[3] = {101, 102, 103};

             printf("First Student ID: %d\n", student_ids[0]);

   return 0;

}
```

Output: First Student ID: 101

Strings store text, like student names:

```
char name[] = "Amit";
```

```
printf("Student: %s\n", name);
```

1.1.5 Pointers

Pointers manage memory directly, a concept I emphasize in my systems programming classes:

```
#include <stdio.h>

int main() {

    int marks = 90;

    int *ptr = &marks;

    printf("Marks: %d, Stored at: %p\n", *ptr, ptr);

    return 0;

}
```

1.1.6 Structures and Unions

Structures group data, like student records:

```
#include <stdio.h>
```

```
struct Student {
    char name[20];
    int roll_no;
};
int main() {
    struct Student s = {"Priya", 101};
        printf("Student: %s, Roll No: %d\n",
s.name, s.roll_no);
    return 0;
}
```

Output: Student: Priya, Roll No: 101

1.1.7 File Handling

Save student data to a file:

```
#include <stdio.h>
int main() {
```

```
    FILE *fp = fopen("students.txt", "w");

    fprintf(fp, "Student: Priya, Marks: 90");

    fclose(fp);

    return 0;

}
```

Practical Exercises:

1. Write a C program to swap two student marks using pointers.

2. Create a structure for student records (name, roll no, marks) and print details for 3 students from my classroom simulation.

3. Count words in a text file containing lecture notes.
   Common Errors: Missing semicolons, uninitialized pointers, array out-of-bounds.

1.2 Introduction to Python

Python's simplicity makes it ideal for scripting and data analysis. Here's a program inspired by a workshop I conducted on student data analysis.

1.2.1 Basics and Data Types

Python uses dynamic typing: `x = 5` (int), `y = 5.5` (float).

Example: Student Report Generator

```
marks = 85

percentage = (marks / 100) * 100

print(f"Student Marks: {marks}, Percentage: {percentage:.2f}%")
```

Output: Student Marks: 85, Percentage: 85.00%

This mirrors a tool I built for quick report generation.

1.2.2 Control Structures

```
marks = 85

if marks >= 90:

    print("Grade: A+")

elif marks >= 80:

    print("Grade: A")

else:

    print("Grade: B or below")
```

Output: Grade: A

1.2.3 Functions

```
def total_marks(subject1, subject2):

    return subject1 + subject2



math, science = 45, 50

print(f"Total Marks: {total_marks(math, science)}")
```

Output: Total Marks: 95

1.2.4 Lists, Tuples, Dictionaries, Sets

List: lst = [1, 2, 3]; lst.append(4)

Tuple: tup = (1, 2, 3) (immutable).

Dict: d = {"name": "John", "age": 30}

Set: s = {1, 2, 3} (no duplicates).

1.2.5 Object-Oriented Programming

```
class Person:

    def __init__(self, name, age):

        self.name = name

        self.age = age

    def display(self):

        print(f"{self.name} is {self.age} years
old")



p = Person("John", 30)
```

```
p.display()  # Output: John is 30 years old
```

1.2.6 File Handling

```
with open("file.txt", "w") as f:
    f.write("Hello, Python!")
```

1.2.7 NumPy and Pandas

NumPy:

```
import numpy as np

arr = np.array([1, 2, 3])

print(arr + 2)  # Output: [3 4 5]
```

Pandas:

```
import pandas as pd

df = pd.DataFrame({"Name": ["John", "Alice"], "Age": [30, 25]})

print(df)
```

Practical Exercises:

Sort a list of numbers using a function.

Use Pandas to compute average marks from a CSV.

Count word frequencies in a file.

Tips: Use virtual environments: python -m venv env; source env/bin/activate (Linux/Mac) or env\Scripts\activate (Windows).

Chapter 2

DATA STRUCTURES AND ALGORITHMS

Focus on implementations in C/Python, with examples from my data management workshops.

2.1 Arrays

Time Complexity: Access O(1), Insert/ Delete O(n).

C:

```
#include <stdio.h>

int main() {

   int arr[5] = {1, 2, 3, 4, 5};

      printf("First element: %d\n", arr[0]);   #
Output: 1

   return 0;
```

```
}
```

Python:

```python
arr = [1, 2, 3, 4, 5]

print(f"First element: {arr[0]}")  # Output: 1
```

2.2 Linked Lists

Singly Linked List (C):

```c
#include <stdio.h>

#include <stdlib.h>

struct Node {

   int data;

   struct Node* next;

};

void insert(struct Node** head, int data) {

          struct Node* newNode = (struct Node*)malloc(sizeof(struct Node));
```

```
    newNode->data = data;
    newNode->next = *head;
    *head = newNode;
}
void printList(struct Node* head) {
    while (head) {
        printf("%d ", head->data);
        head = head->next;
    }
}
int main() {
    struct Node* head = NULL;
    insert(&head, 1); insert(&head, 2);
    printList(head);  // Output: 2 1
```

```
    return 0;
}
```

Python:

```python
class Node:
    def __init__(self, data):
        self.data = data
        self.next = None
class LinkedList:
    def __init__(self):
        self.head = None
    def insert(self, data):
        new_node = Node(data)
        new_node.next = self.head
        self.head = new_node
```

```
    def display(self):
        temp = self.head
        while temp:
            print(temp.data, end=" ")
            temp = temp.next
ll = LinkedList()
ll.insert(1); ll.insert(2)
ll.display()  # Output: 2 1
```

2.3 Stacks and Queues

Stack:

```
stack = []
stack.append(1)  # Push
print(stack.pop())  # Output: 1
```

Queue:

```
from collections import deque
```

```
queue = deque()

queue.append(1)  # Enqueue

print(queue.popleft())  # Output: 1
```

2.4 Trees

BST (Python):

```
class Node:

    def __init__(self, data):

        self.data = data

        self.left = None

        self.right = None

def inorder(root):

    if root:

        inorder(root.left)

        print(root.data, end=" ")

        inorder(root.right)
```

```
root = Node(1)

root.left = Node(2)

root.right = Node(3)

inorder(root)  # Output: 2 1 3
```

2.5 Graphs

BFS (Python):

```
from collections import deque

def bfs(graph, start):

    visited = set()

    queue = deque([start])

    visited.add(start)

    while queue:

        vertex = queue.popleft()

        print(vertex, end=" ")

        for neighbor in graph[vertex]:
```

```
            if neighbor not in visited:
                visited.add(neighbor)
                queue.append(neighbor)

graph = {0: [1, 2], 1: [0, 3], 2: [0, 3], 3: [1,
2]}
bfs(graph, 0)  # Output: 0 1 2 3
```

2.6 Sorting and Searching

Bubble Sort:

```
def bubble_sort(arr):
    n = len(arr)
    for i in range(n):
        for j in range(0, n-i-1):
            if arr[j] > arr[j+1]:
                arr[j], arr[j+1] = arr[j+1], arr[j]
    return arr
```

```
print(bubble_sort([5, 3, 8, 1]))  # Output: [1, 3, 5, 8]
```

Binary Search:

```
def binary_search(arr, target):
    left, right = 0, len(arr)-1
    while left <= right:
        mid = (left + right) // 2
        if arr[mid] == target:
            return mid
        elif arr[mid] < target:
            left = mid + 1
        else:
            right = mid - 1
    return -1
```

Exercises: Implement BST in C; Sort a list in Python with a classroom score example.

Chapter 3

DISCRETE MATHEMATICS

3.1 Sets

Operations: Union ($A \cup B$), Intersection ($A \cap B$).

Example: $A = \{1,2\}$, $B = \{2,3\}$; $A \cup B = \{1,2,3\}$.

3.2 Relations and Functions

Relations: Subset of $A \times B$.

Functions: Injective, Surjective.

3.3 Logic

De Morgan's: $\neg(A \land B) = \neg A \lor \neg B$.

3.4 Graph Theory

Eulerian Path: Traverses all edges once.

3.5 Combinatorics

Combinations: $C(n,k) = n! / (k!(n-k)!)$.

Example: $C(5,3) = 10$.

Exercises: Prove De Morgan's; Calculate

permutations for scheduling problems in my classes.

Chapter 4

COMPUTER ORGANIZATION AND ARCHITECTURE

4.1 Basic Structure

Components: CPU, Memory, I/O.

4.2 CPU

ALU: Arithmetic/Logic.

Registers: PC, IR.

4.3 Memory Hierarchy

Cache, RAM, Secondary.

4.4 I/O Systems

Interrupts, DMA.

4.5 Addressing Modes

Immediate, Direct, Indirect.

4.6 Pipelining

Fetch, Decode, Execute.

Exercises: Simulate CPU cycle in a simple

processor model I used in lectures; Compare addressing modes.

Chapter 5

DATABASE MANAGEMENT SYSTEMS (DBMS)

5.1 Relational Model

Keys: Primary, Foreign.

5.2 ER Diagrams

Entities, Relationships.

5.3 Normalization

1NF, 2NF, 3NF, BCNF.

5.4 SQL

```
CREATE TABLE Students (
    ID INT PRIMARY KEY,
    Name VARCHAR(50),
    Age INT
);
```

INSERT INTO Students VALUES (1, 'John', 20);

SELECT * FROM Students WHERE Age > 18;

5.5 Transactions

ACID properties.

Exercises: Normalize a student database table; Write SQL joins for class records.

Chapter 6:

ELECTIVE - WEB TECHNOLOGIES

6.1 HTML

```
<!DOCTYPE html>

<html>

<head><title>Hello 2025</title></head>

<body><h1>Hello, Web!</h1><p>Exploring 2025 trends.</p></body>

</html>
```

6.2 CSS

```
body { background-color: lightblue; }

h1 { color: white; text-align: center; }
```

6.3 JavaScript

```
function greet() { alert("Hello, 2025 Web!");
}
```

Exercises: Build a webpage with form validation for a student registration system.

Chapter 7

LABS AND PRACTICAL TRAINING

Labs:

C/Python: Implement factorial with error checking.

Data Structures: Stack for undo operations in a text editor simulation.

DBMS: SQLite queries for student databases.

Mini-Projects:

Library Management System: SQLite + Python GUI for book tracking.

Tic-Tac-Toe: Array-based game with AI hints.

Student Record System: Linked list in C for class rosters.

Calculator: Python functions with history log.

Notepad: Tkinter GUI with save features.

Inclusive Tip: Use screen readers (NVDA, VoiceOver) for testing accessibility.

Part 2

SYSTEMS AND SOFTWARE DEVELOPMENT

PREFACE TO PART 2

Focuses on Java, operating systems, networks, software engineering, and probability/statistics, with AI/ML elective. Updated for 2025 tools like JDK 24.

Chapter 0

SETTING UP YOUR ENVIRONMENT

JDK: 24+ (https://openjdk.org/).

Python Libraries: pip install scipy statsmodels scikit-learn tensorflow.

Test: Compile Java "Hello, World!" with 2025 updates.

Chapter 1

OBJECT-ORIENTED PROGRAMMING (JAVA)

1.1 Classes and Objects

```
public class Person {

    String name;

    int age;

    public Person(String name, int age) {

        this.name = name;

        this.age = age;

    }

    public void display() {

        System.out.println(name + " is " + age);

    }
```

```
}
```

1.2 Inheritance

```
public class Employee extends Person {
    double salary;
        public Employee(String name, int age, double salary) {
        super(name, age);
        this.salary = salary;
    }
}
```

1.3 Exception Handling

```
try {
    int x = 10 / 0;
} catch (ArithmeticException e) {
```

```
        System.out.println("Error: " +
e.getMessage());
}
```

Exercises: Create vehicle hierarchy; Handle exceptions in a payroll system.

Chapter 2

OPERATING SYSTEMS

2.1 Processes and Threads

```
class MyThread extends Thread {
   public void run() {
        System.out.println("Thread running in 2025 OS simulation");
   }
}
```

2.2 Scheduling

FCFS simulation in Python.

2.3 Memory Management

Paging, Virtual Memory.

2.4 File Systems

```
import java.io.*;
```

```
try (BufferedWriter writer = new
BufferedWriter(new FileWriter("file.txt"))) {

   writer.write("Hello, OS! 2025 edition.");

}
```

Exercises: Simulate Round-Robin for task management; Producer-consumer problem.

Chapter 3

COMPUTER NETWORKS

3.1 OSI Model

Layers: Physical to Application.

3.2 Protocols

TCP/UDP, HTTP.

3.3 Socket Programming

Server:

```
import java.net.*;

import java.io.*;

ServerSocket server = new
ServerSocket(8080);

Socket client = server.accept();

BufferedReader in = new
BufferedReader(new
```

```
InputStreamReader(client.getInputStream())
);

System.out.println(in.readLine());
```

Exercises: Build a chat app for remote collaboration.

Chapter 4

SOFTWARE ENGINEERING

4.1 SDLC

Agile, Waterfall.

4.2 Testing

```
import org.junit.Test;

import static org.junit.Assert.assertEquals;

public class TestAdd {

    @Test

    public void test() {

        assertEquals(4, 2 + 2);

    }

}
```

Exercises: Draw UML for a project management tool; Write tests.

Chapter 5

PROBABILITY AND STATISTICS

5.1 Probability

Bayes' Theorem.

5.2 Distributions

```
import scipy.stats as stats

print(stats.norm.pdf(0))
```

5.3 Inference

Hypothesis Testing.

Exercises: Compute probabilities for risk assessment; t-test on dataset.

Chapter 6

ELECTIVE - INTRODUCTION TO AI/ML

6.1 Machine Learning

```
from sklearn.ensemble import RandomForestClassifier

from sklearn.datasets import load_iris

from sklearn.model_selection import train_test_split

iris = load_iris()

X_train, X_test, y_train, y_test = train_test_split(iris.data, iris.target, test_size=0.2)

clf = RandomForestClassifier().fit(X_train, y_train)

print(clf.score(X_test, y_test))
```

Exercises: Implement KNN; Discuss AI ethics in 2025 contexts like agentic AI.

Chapter 7

LABS AND PRACTICAL TRAINING

Labs: Java threads, network sockets.

Mini-Projects: Banking system with security, data analyzer using ML.

Part 3

ADVANCED AND SPECIALIZED TOPICS

PREFACE TO PART 3

Covers advanced DBMS, AI/ML, cybersecurity, cloud computing, with Data Science elective. Updated for 2025 like MongoDB 8.1.

Chapter 0

SETTING UP YOUR ENVIRONMENT

MongoDB: 8.1 (https://www.mongodb.com/).

AWS CLI: Latest v2 (https://aws.amazon.com/cli/).

Libraries: pip install matplotlib seaborn pymongo boto3.

Chapter 1

ADVANCED DBMS AND DATA ANALYTICS

1.1 NoSQL

```
import pymongo

client = pymongo.MongoClient("mongodb://localhost:27017/")

db = client["school"]

students = db["students"]

students.insert_one({"name": "Alice", "age": 20})
```

1.2 Analytics

```
import pandas as pd

df = pd.DataFrame({"Name": ["Alice", "Bob"], "Marks": [85, 90]})
```

```
print(df["Marks"].mean())
```

1.3 SQL Advanced

```
SELECT Name, Marks, RANK() OVER (ORDER BY Marks DESC) AS Rank
FROM Students;
```

Exercises: MongoDB queries for student data; Visualize analytics.

Chapter 2

ARTIFICIAL INTELLIGENCE AND MACHINE LEARNING

2.1 ML

```
from sklearn.ensemble import
RandomForestClassifier

clf = RandomForestClassifier().fit(X_train,
y_train)
```

2.2 Neural Networks

```
import tensorflow as tf

model =
tf.keras.Sequential([tf.keras.layers.Dense(1,
input_shape=(1,))])

model.compile(optimizer='sgd', loss='mse')

model.fit([1,2,3], [2,4,6], epochs=100)
```

Exercises: Train classifier on iris dataset; Analyze bias in AI models.

Chapter 3

CYBERSECURITY

3.1 Encryption

```
import hashlib

password = "secure123"

hashed =
hashlib.sha256(password.encode()).hexdiges
t()

print(hashed)
```

3.2 Secure Coding

Parameterized SQL.

Exercises: Implement AES for data protection; Simulate firewall rules.

Chapter 4

CLOUD COMPUTING

4.1 AWS

```
import boto3

s3 = boto3.client('s3')

s3.upload_file('file.txt', 'mybucket', 'file.txt')
```

4.2 Microservices

```
from flask import Flask

app = Flask(__name__)

@app.route('/')

def hello(): return "Microservice in 2025"
```

Exercises: Deploy Flask app to cloud.

Chapter 5

ELECTIVE - DATA SCIENCE

5.1 Wrangling

```
import pandas as pd

df = pd.DataFrame({"A": [1, None, 3], "B": [4, 5, 6]})

df.fillna(df.mean(), inplace=True)
```

5.2 Visualization

```
import seaborn as sns

sns.scatterplot(x="A", y="B", data=df)
```

Exercises: Clean dataset; Build predictive model.

Chapter 6

LABS AND PRACTICAL TRAINING

Labs: AI training, cloud deployment.

Mini-Projects: E-Commerce DB with NoSQL, secure login system.

Part 4

CAPSTONE AND EMERGING INNOVATIONS

PREFACE TO PART 4

Focuses on electives, major project, and seminar, incorporating 2025 trends like post-quantum cryptography.

Chapter 0

SETTING UP YOUR ENVIRONMENT

Qiskit: 2.1.1 (pip install qiskit).

React: npx create-react-app my-app.

Chapter 1

ELECTIVE I - ADVANCED AI AND DEEP LEARNING

1.1 Deep Learning

```
import tensorflow as tf

model = tf.keras.Sequential([

    tf.keras.layers.Conv2D(32, (3, 3), activation='relu', input_shape=(28, 28, 1)),

    tf.keras.layers.Dense(10, activation='softmax')

])
```

1.2 Ethical AI

```
import shap

explainer = shap.TreeExplainer(model)

shap_values = explainer.shap_values(X)
```

Exercises: Train CNN; Analyze bias in agentic AI systems.

Chapter 2

ELECTIVE II - QUANTUM COMPUTING BASICS

2.1 Qiskit

```
from qiskit import QuantumCircuit, Aer, execute

qc = QuantumCircuit(2, 2)

qc.h(0)

qc.cx(0, 1)

qc.measure([0, 1], [0, 1])

simulator = Aer.get_backend('qasm_simulator')

result = execute(qc, simulator).result()

print(result.get_counts())
```

Exercises: Build quantum circuit for entanglement demo.

Chapter 3

MAJOR PROJECT/ INTERNSHIP

Sample: AI Healthcare App with React, Flask, TensorFlow 2.19, AWS.

Exercises: Write proposal; Deploy app with post-quantum security.

Chapter 4

SEMINAR - 2025 IT TRENDS

Topics: Agentic AI, post-quantum cryptography, spatial computing, sustainable IT, 6G.

Exercises: Create presentation on quantum impacts.

Chapter 5

LABS AND PRACTICAL TRAINING

Labs: CNN training, quantum circuit simulation.

Mini-Projects: AI chatbot with ethical safeguards, blockchain wallet for secure transactions.

Appendix

CAREER PATHWAYS AND CERTIFICATIONS

Roles: Software Developer, AI Engineer, Cloud Architect.

Certifications: AWS Certified Solutions Architect, CEH, Google ML Engineer, IBM Quantum Developer.

Tips: Build portfolio, use LinkedIn for networking in 2025 job market.

INDEX

GLOSSARY

Qubit: Quantum bit with superposition.

Zero-Trust: Security model verifying all requests.

Agentic AI: AI systems that act autonomously.

REFERENCES

Kernighan, B. W., & Ritchie, D. M. (1988). The C Programming Language. Prentice Hall.

Goodfellow, I., Bengio, Y., & Courville, A. (2016). Deep Learning. MIT Press.

Silberschatz, A., Galvin, P. B., & Gagne, G. (2018). Operating System Concepts. Wiley.

Industry reports: Gartner Top 10 Strategic Technology Trends for 2025, McKinsey Technology Trends Outlook 2025, IBM Quantum Technology Monitor 2025.

9 788199 262300

Printed at Repro India Ltd.